PUN INTENDED

Published by Willow Creek Press, Inc.
P.O. Box 147, Minocqua, Wisconsin 54548

Printed in the United States

PUN INTENDED

OVER 300 OF THE "PUNNIEST" JOKES OF ALL TIME.

WILLOW CREEK PRESS®

I HATE RUSSIAN
DOLLS, THEY'RE
SO FULL OF
THEMSELVES.

TWO ANTENNAS
MET, FELL IN LOVE
AND EVENTUALLY
GOT MARRIED. THE
WEDDING CEREMONY
WASN'T MUCH BUT
THE RECEPTION
WAS EXCELLENT.

NEED AN ARK?
I NOAH GUY.

MY WIFE WARNED
ME NOT TO STEAL
THE KITCHEN
UTENSILS, BUT
IT'S A WHISK I'M
WILLING TO TAKE.

AFTER MANUALLY
ROTATING THE
HEAVY MACHINERY,
THE WORKER GREW
PRETTY CRANKY.

DON'T SPELL PART
BACKWARDS.
IT'S A TRAP.

I WASN'T ORIGINALLY GOING TO GET A BRAIN TRANSPLANT, BUT THEN I CHANGED MY MIND.

ELVES ARE ALWAYS DEFENDING THE SHAPE OF THEIR EARS. THEY MAKE SOME GOOD POINTS.

I USED TO BE ADDICTED TO SOAP, BUT I'M CLEAN NOW.

DID YOU HEAR THE
JOKE ABOUT THE
PEANUT BUTTER?

I'M NOT TELLING
YOU. YOU MIGHT
SPREAD IT!

A LAWYER-TURNED
COOK IS A SUE CHEF.

CLEANING MIRRORS
IS A JOB I COULD
REALLY SEE
MYSELF DOING.

GOATS IN FRANCE ARE
GREAT MUSICIANS
BECAUSE THEY HAVE
FRENCH HORNS.

"YOUR FINEST
SCOTCH, PLEASE."

"YES, SIR," THE GUY
AT STAPLES SAYS AS HE
HANDS ME A 12 YEAR
OLD ROLL OF TAPE.

WHITE BOARDS ARE
REMARKABLE.

MY SNOWBOARDING
SKILLS ARE
REALLY GOING
DOWNHILL FAST!

6:30 IS THE BEST
TIME ON A CLOCK...
HANDS DOWN.

POLICE HAVE ARRESTED
THE WORLD
TONGUE-TWISTER
CHAMPION. I IMAGINE
HE'LL BE GIVEN A
TOUGH SENTENCE.

A NEW YEAR'S
RESOLUTION IS
SOMETHING THAT
GOES IN ONE YEAR
AND OUT THE OTHER.

I TRIED TO FINISH
THE LEFTOVERS,
BUT MY PLANS
WERE FOILED.

I HAVE A SPEED
BUMP PHOBIA
BUT I'M SLOWLY
GETTING OVER IT.

THE MAN'S
ZIPPER BROKE,
BUT HE FIXED
IT ON THE FLY.

SOMEONE RIPPED SOME
PAGES OUT OF BOTH
ENDS OF MY DICTIONARY
TODAY. IT JUST GOES
FROM BAD TO WORSE!

DID YOU KNOW
TALLER PEOPLE
SLEEP LONGER
IN BED?

MOST PEOPLE HAVE
32 TEETH. SOME
JUST HAVE 8.

IT'S SIMPLE METH.

WHEN MAKING
BUTTER THERE IS
LITTLE MARGARINE
FOR ERROR.

I THOUGHT ABOUT
BECOMING A WITCH,
SO I TRIED IT OUT
FOR A SPELL.

MOST PEOPLE ARE
SHOCKED WHEN
THEY FIND OUT
HOW BAD I AM AS
AN ELECTRICIAN.

I GOT THROWN OUT
OF MATH CLASS
FOR ONE TOO MANY
INFRACTIONS.

TREE TRIMMERS DO
SUCH A FANTASTIC
JOB, THEY SHOULD
TAKE A BOUGH.

IT'S HARD TO
EXPLAIN PUNS TO
KLEPTOMANIACS
BECAUSE THEY ALWAYS
TAKE THINGS LITERALLY.

A COURTROOM ARTIST
WAS ARRESTED TODAY
FOR AN UNKNOWN
REASON... DETAILS
ARE SKETCHY.

DON'T TRUST
ATOMS, THEY MAKE
UP EVERYTHING.

SKUNKS LOVE
VALENTINE'S DAY
BECAUSE THEY ARE
VERY SCENT-IMENTAL.

SOMEONE THREW
CHEESE AT ME.
REAL MATURE!

"DOCTOR, THERE'S A
PATIENT ON LINE 1 THAT
SAYS HE'S INVISIBLE."

"WELL, TELL HIM I CAN'T
SEE HIM RIGHT NOW."

MY BOSS IS GOING
TO FIRE THE
EMPLOYEE WITH THE
WORST POSTURE. I
HAVE A HUNCH, IT
MIGHT BE ME.

I WAS ADDICTED TO THE
HOKEY POKEY... BUT
THANKFULLY, I TURNED
MYSELF AROUND.

ON THE OTHER
HAND, YOU HAVE
DIFFERENT FINGERS.

I'M TAKING PART IN
A STAIR CLIMBING
COMPETITION. GUESS
I BETTER STEP
UP MY GAME.

AS A SCARECROW,
PEOPLE SAY I'M
OUTSTANDING IN
MY FIELD. BUT HAY,
IT'S IN MY JEANS.

I HATE INSECT
PUNS, THEY
REALLY BUG ME.

SOMETIMES I TUCK
MY KNEES INTO MY
CHEST AND LEAN
FORWARD. THAT'S
JUST HOW I ROLL.

IF SATAN EVER LOST HIS
HAIR, THERE WOULD
BE HELL TOUPEE.

JUSTICE IS A DISH
BEST SERVED COLD
BECAUSE IF IT WERE
SERVED WARM, IT
WOULD BE JUST WATER.

I BOUGHT SOME SHOES
FROM A DRUG DEALER.
I DON'T KNOW WHAT
HE LACED THEM
WITH, BUT I'VE BEEN
TRIPPING ALL DAY.

WAKING UP IN
THE MORNING IS
AN EYE-OPENING
EXPERIENCE.

THINGS MADE IN
AUSTRALIA ARE
HIGH KOALA-TY.

LEARNING HOW TO
COLLECT TRASH
WASN'T THAT HARD.
I JUST PICKED IT UP
AS I WENT ALONG.

PIG PUNS ARE
REALLY BOARING.

TWO HATS WERE
HANGING ON A HAT
RACK IN THE HALLWAY.

ONE HAT SAID TO THE
OTHER, "YOU STAY HERE;
I'LL GO ON A HEAD."

THE RACE CAR DRIVER
HAD A PRETTY
CHECKERED PAST...

YESTERDAY I
ACCIDENTALLY
SWALLOWED SOME
FOOD COLORING.
THE DOCTOR SAYS
I'M OK, BUT I FEEL
LIKE I'VE DYED A
LITTLE INSIDE.

A CARDBOARD
BELT WOULD BE A
WAIST OF PAPER.

MY EX-WIFE STILL
MISSES ME, BUT HER
AIM IS STEADILY
IMPROVING.

HAVE YOU EVER
TRIED TO EAT A
CLOCK? IT'S VERY
TIME-CONSUMING.

MY GRANDMA IS
HAVING TROUBLE
WITH HER NEW STAIR
LIFT. IT'S DRIVING
HER UP THE WALL.

A SMALL BOY SWALLOWED SOME COINS AND WAS TAKEN TO THE HOSPITAL. WHEN HIS GRANDMOTHER TELEPHONED TO ASK HOW HE WAS, THE NURSE SAID "NO CHANGE YET."

CORDUROY PILLOWS ARE MAKING HEADLINES.

JOKES ABOUT GERMAN SAUSAGE ARE THE WURST.

MY DOG MINTON
ATE ALL MY
SHUTTLECOCKS.
BAD MINTON!

I'VE JUST BEEN ON A
ONCE-IN-A-LIFETIME
HOLIDAY. I'LL
TELL YOU WHAT,
NEVER AGAIN.

PENCILS COULD BE
MADE WITH ERASERS AT
BOTH ENDS, BUT WHAT
WOULD BE THE POINT?

IT'S A LENGTHY
ARTICLE ON JAPANESE
SWORD FIGHTERS
BUT I CAN SAMURAIS
IT FOR YOU.

I QUIT GYMNASTICS
BECAUSE I WAS FED
UP OF HANGING
AROUND THE BARS.

TO THE GUY
WHO INVENTED
ZERO: THANKS
FOR NOTHING!

I USED TO BE A
TRAIN DRIVER BUT I
GOT SIDETRACKED.

WHEN I FINALLY
WORKED OUT THE
SECRET TO CLONING, I
WAS BESIDE MYSELF.

I RECENTLY HEARD
ABOUT A MANNEQUIN
THAT LOST ALL
OF HIS FRIENDS
BECAUSE HE WAS SO
CLOTHES MINDED!

IF A JUDGE LOVES
THE SOUND OF HIS
OWN VOICE, EXPECT
A LONG SENTENCE.

I LEFT MY LAST
BOYFRIEND BECAUSE
HE WOULDN'T
STOP COUNTING.
I WONDER WHAT
HE'S UP TO NOW.

HUNG A PICTURE UP
ON THE WALL THE
OTHER DAY. NAILED IT.

SOMEONE BROKE
INTO MY HOUSE LAST
NIGHT AND STOLE MY
LIMBO STICK. HOW
LOW CAN YOU GET?

THE MAN WHO
HAD FALLEN IN AN
UPHOLSTERY FACTORY
IS NOW SAID TO BE
FULLY RECOVERED.

READING WHILE
SUNBATHING MAKES
YOU WELL RED.

I WOULDN'T BUY ANYTHING WITH VELCRO. IT'S A TOTAL RIP-OFF.

WHEN THE CANNIBAL SHOWED UP LATE FOR LUNCH, THE OTHERS GAVE HIM THE COLD SHOULDER.

I WAS HAPPY WITH MY HISTORIAN JOB UNTIL I REALIZED THERE WAS NO FUTURE IN IT.

ONCE YOU HAVE
SEEN ONE SHOPPING
CENTER, YOU'VE
SEEN A MALL.

THE FIRST TIME I
GOT A UNIVERSAL
REMOTE CONTROL, I
THOUGHT TO MYSELF
"THIS CHANGES
EVERYTHING."

I FEAR MOVING
STAIRS IS
ESCALATING.

I WENT TO A REALLY
EMOTIONAL WEDDING
THE OTHER DAY. EVEN
THE CAKE WAS IN TIERS.

I TRIED TO BE A
TAILOR, BUT I WASN'T
SUITED FOR IT...
MAINLY BECAUSE IT
WAS A SO-SO JOB.

I RELISH THE FACT
THAT YOU'VE MUSTARD
THE STRENGTH TO
KETCHUP TO ME.

MY FIRST JOB WAS
WORKING IN AN ORANGE
JUICE FACTORY, BUT I
GOT CANNED: COULDN'T
CONCENTRATE.

MY SISTER WAS
ENGAGED TO A MAN
WITH A WOODEN LEG
BUT SHE BROKE IT OFF.

I TOLD MY FRIEND
10 JOKES TO GET HIM
TO LAUGH. SADLY,
NO PUN IN 10 DID.

I HAD A NECK BRACE
FITTED YEARS AGO
AND I'VE NEVER
LOOKED BACK SINCE.

MY MOM JUST FOUND OUT
THAT I'VE REPLACED HER
BED WITH A TRAMPOLINE.
SHE HIT THE ROOF.

THREE CONSPIRACY
THEORISTS WALK INTO
A BAR. YOU CAN'T
TELL ME THAT'S JUST
A COINCIDENCE!

HAVE YOU EVER
HEARD OF AN
HONEST CHEETAH?

I BOUGHT A DICTIONARY
AND WHEN I GOT HOME
I REALIZED ALL THE
PAGES WERE BLANK;
I HAVE NO WORDS FOR
HOW ANGRY I AM.

TELLING A
DEMOLITIONIST
HOW TO DO HIS JOB
IS DESTRUCTIVE
CRITICISM.

I ACCIDENTALLY HANDED MY WIFE A GLUE STICK INSTEAD OF A CHAP STICK. SHE STILL ISN'T TALKING TO ME.

BROKEN PUPPETS FOR SALE. NO STRINGS ATTACHED.

A LOT OF PEOPLE CRY WHEN THEY CUT ONIONS. THE TRICK IS NOT TO FORM AN EMOTIONAL BOND.

A TERMITE WALKS
INTO A BAR AND
SAYS, "WHERE IS
THE BAR TENDER?"

I ACCIDENTALLY WENT
TO BED WITH MY
CONTACT LENSES IN
THE OTHER NIGHT. MY
DREAMS HAVE NEVER
BEEN CLEARER.

HE BROKE INTO SONG
WHEN HE COULDN'T
FIND THE KEY.

A FRIEND OF MINE TRIED
TO ANNOY ME WITH
BIRD PUNS, BUT I SOON
REALIZED THAT TOUCAN
PLAY AT THAT GAME.

I TRIED TO BE A CHEF-
FIGURED IT WOULD ADD
A LITTLE SPICE TO MY
LIFE, BUT I JUST DIDN'T
HAVE THE THYME.

SEA CAPTAINS
DON'T LIKE
CREW CUTS.

I HAD TO QUIT MY
JOB AT THE SHOE
RECYCLING FACTORY.
IT WAS JUST TOO
SOLE DESTROYING.

TWO SILK WORMS
HAD A RACE. THEY
ENDED UP IN A TIE.

MY FRIEND MADE
A JOKE ABOUT A
TV CONTROLLER.
IT WASN'T
REMOTELY FUNNY.

I WENT TO A BUFFET DINNER WITH MY NEIGHBOR, WHO IS A TAXIDERMIST. AFTER SUCH A BIG MEAL, I WAS STUFFED.

A GOLF BALL IS A GOLF BALL NO MATTER HOW YOU PUTT IT.

I USED TO HAVE A FEAR OF HURDLES, BUT I GOT OVER IT.

I THOUGHT I SAW AN
EYE DOCTOR ON AN
ALASKAN ISLAND, BUT
IT TURNED OUT TO BE
AN OPTICAL ALEUTIAN.

WHEN IT CAME TO
GETTING EVEN
WITH MY LOCAL BUS
COMPANY, I PULLED
OUT ALL THE STOPS.

WHENEVER I FEEL
BLUE, I START
BREATHING AGAIN.

A MAN JUST ASSAULTED ME WITH MILK, CREAM AND BUTTER. HOW DAIRY.

A SIGN ON THE LAWN AT A DRUG REHAB CENTER SAID, "KEEP OFF THE GRASS."

I CAN HEAR MUSIC COMING OUT FROM MY PRINTER. I THINK THE PAPER'S JAMMIN' AGAIN...

I WENT TO A RESTAURANT LAST NIGHT AND HAD THE WOOKIE STEAK. IT WAS A LITTLE CHEWY.

DON'T TRUST PEOPLE THAT DO ACUPUNCTURE, THEY'RE BACK STABBERS.

POLICE WERE CALLED TO A DAYCARE CENTER WHERE A THREE-YEAR-OLD WAS RESISTING A REST.

PEOPLE WHO LACK
THE PATIENCE
FOR CALLIGRAPHY
WILL NEVER HAVE
PROPERLY FORMED
CHARACTERS.

COFFEE IS THE
SILENT VICTIM IN
OUR HOUSE. IT GETS
MUGGED EVERY DAY.

MY CEILING ISN'T
THE BEST... BUT
IT'S UP THERE!

NOBODY EVER ASKS HOW COCA-COLA IS DOING. IT'S ALWAYS, "IS PEPSI OKAY?"

TWO PEANUTS ARE WALKING DOWN THE STREET. ONE IS ASSAULTED.

SOME PEOPLE LOVE EGGNOG, WHILE OTHERS FIND IT'S NOT ALL IT'S CRACKED UP TO BE.

MY SISTER BET ME
$100 THAT I COULDN'T
BUILD A WORKING CAR
OUT OF SPAGHETTI. YOU
SHOULD'VE SEEN HER
FACE AS I DROVE PASTA.

I LOVE CANDY CANES
WHEN THEY'RE IN
MINT CONDITION.

I ORDERED 2000
POUNDS OF
CHINESE SOUP.
IT WAS WON TON.

SINGING IN THE SHOWER
IS ALL FUN AND GAMES
UNTIL YOU GET SHAMPOO
IN YOUR MOUTH. THEN IT
BECOMES A SOAP OPERA.

THIS GIRL SAID SHE
RECOGNIZED ME FROM
THE VEGETARIAN
CLUB BUT I'VE NEVER
SEEN HERBIVORE.

A PLATEAU IS THE
HIGHEST FORM
OF FLATTERY.

I OWE A LOT TO THE
SIDEWALKS. THEY'VE
BEEN KEEPING ME
OFF THE STREETS
FOR YEARS.

DR.'S ARE SAYING NOT
TO WORRY ABOUT THE
BIRD FLU BECAUSE
IT'S TWEETABLE.

I'D TELL YOU A
CHEMISTRY JOKE BUT
I KNOW I WOULDN'T
GET A REACTION.

I JUST WATCHED
A PROGRAM ABOUT
BEAVERS. IT WAS THE
BEST DAM PROGRAM
I'VE EVER SEEN.

SANTA OWES A LOT TO
HIS LITTLE HELPERS.
ONE MIGHT SAY HE'S
AN ELF-MADE MAN.

IF A DOG WAS A
COMPUTER, WOULD
ITS BARK BE BIGGER
THAN ITS BYTE?

I WAS SO SAD AND
CRYING WHEN I LOST
MY VIDEO GAME
BUT UNFORTUNATELY,
THERE WAS NOBODY
TO CONSOLE ME.

I WAS GOING TO SHARE
A VEGETABLE JOKE BUT
IT'S TOO CORNY.

WHEN MY ICE
HOUSE FALLS
APART IGLOO IT
BACK TOGETHER.

IF LIFE THROWS
YOU MELONS...
YOU MIGHT BE
DYSLEXIC.

I'M READING A
HORROR STORY IN
BRAILLE. SOMETHING
BAD IS ABOUT
TO HAPPEN... I
CAN FEEL IT.

CAN FEBRUARY
MARCH? NO, BUT
APRIL MAY!

I NEED TO STOP
DRINKING SO MUCH
MILK. IT'S AN
UDDER DISGRACE.

I TRIED TO SUE THE
AIRLINE FOR LOSING
MY LUGGAGE. I
LOST MY CASE.

I USED TO BUILD
STAIRS FOR A
LIVING, IT'S AN
UP AND DOWN
BUSINESS.

MATHEMATICIANS
ARE SUM
WORSHIPERS.

THEY'RE BUILDING A
RESTAURANT ON MARS
NOW. THEY SAY THE
FOOD WILL BE GREAT,
BUT THEY'RE WORRIED
ABOUT THE LACK OF
ATMOSPHERE.

I USED TO BE A
BANKER, BUT THEN
I LOST INTEREST.

I WORK IN A PAPER FACTORY, WHERE MY RESPONSIBILITIES ARE TWOFOLD.

SOMEONE STOLE MY MOOD RING. I'M NOT SURE HOW I FEEL ABOUT THAT.

I TRIED TO ESCAPE THE APPLE STORE. I COULDN'T BECAUSE THERE WERE NO WINDOWS.

THE FUTURE, THE
PRESENT AND THE
PAST WALKED INTO
A BAR. THINGS GOT
A LITTLE TENSE.

JOKES ABOUT
UNEMPLOYED
PEOPLE ARE NOT
FUNNY. THEY JUST
DON'T WORK.

I FEAR MY STUTTERING
BROTHER MAY NEVER
FINISH HIS PRISON
SENTENCE.

R.I.P BOILED
WATER. YOU WILL
BE MIST.

WHERE SHOULD A
DOG GO WHEN IT'S
LOST ITS TAIL?

THE RETAIL STORE
OF COURSE.

TWO WI-FI ANTENNAS
GOT MARRIED
LAST SATURDAY.
THE RECEPTION
WAS FANTASTIC.

CLAUSTROPHOBIC
PEOPLE ARE MORE
PRODUCTIVE THINKING
OUT OF THE BOX.

THIS MORNING SOME
CLOWN OPENED
THE DOOR FOR
ME. I THOUGHT TO
MYSELF THAT'S A
NICE JESTER.

MY SISTER WAS
CRYING SO I ASKED
HER IF SHE WAS
HAVING A CRY-SIS.

A COP JUST KNOCKED
ON MY DOOR AND
TOLD ME THAT MY
DOGS WERE CHASING
PEOPLE ON BIKES.
MY DOGS DON'T
EVEN OWN BIKES...

I'VE DECIDED TO
SELL MY HOOVER...
IT WAS JUST
COLLECTING DUST.

ZEBRAS ARE JUST
HORSES THAT ESCAPED
FROM PRISON.

I RAN OUT OF POKER CHIPS SO I USED DRY FRUITS FOR PLAYING INSTEAD. PEOPLE WENT NUTS WHEN THEY SAW ME RAISIN THE STAKES.

I'M GLAD I KNOW SIGN LANGUAGE, IT'S PRETTY HANDY.

I WENT TO A SEAFOOD DISCO LAST WEEK... AND PULLED A MUSSEL.

I WANTED TO TELL
YOU A JOKE ABOUT
LEECHES, BUT
THEY ALL SUCK.

I FOUND A ROCK
YESTERDAY WHICH
MEASURED 1760
YARDS IN LENGTH.
MUST BE SOME KIND
OF MILESTONE.

WHAT IF THERE WERE
NO HYPOTHETICAL
QUESTIONS?

I GOT A JOB IN A
HEALTH CLUB, BUT
THEY SAID I WASN'T
FIT FOR THE JOB.

THIS MAY COME
ACROSS AS CHEESY
BUT I THINK
YOU'RE GRATE.

I WAITED AND STAYED
UP ALL NIGHT TO
FIGURE OUT WHERE
THE SUN GOES. THEN
IT DAWNED ON ME.

CONFUCIUS SAY,
MAN WHO RUNS
BEHIND CAR WILL
GET EXHAUSTED,
BUT MAN WHO RUNS
IN FRONT OF CAR
WILL GET TIRED.

NO MATTER HOW
MUCH YOU PUSH THE
ENVELOPE, IT'LL STILL
BE STATIONERY.

FISHERMEN ARE
REEL MEN.

I WENT TO SEE
THE LIBERTY BELL
THE OTHER DAY.
IT'S NOT ALL IT'S
CRACKED UP TO BE.

MY LANDLORD SAYS HE
NEEDS TO COME TALK
TO ME ABOUT HOW HIGH
MY HEATING BILL IS. I
TOLD HIM, "MY DOOR
IS ALWAYS OPEN."

WHICH BEES PRODUCE
MILK? THE BOO-BEES!

THE GUY WHO
INVENTED THROAT
LOZENGES DIES
LAST WEEK. THERE
WAS NO COFFIN AT
THE FUNERAL.

I WANTED TO LEARN
TO DRIVE STICK
SHIFT, BUT I COULDN'T
FIND A MANUAL.

REMAINS TO BE SEEN
IF GLASS COFFINS
BECOME POPULAR.

I BOUGHT THE WORLD'S WORST THESAURUS YESTERDAY. NOT ONLY IS IT TERRIBLE, IT'S TERRIBLE.

DID YOU HEAR ABOUT THE SICK ITALIAN CHEF?

UNFORTUNATELY, HE PASTAWAY.

WANNA GO ON A PICNIC? ALPACA LUNCH.

HACKERS BROUGHT
DOWN MY ONLINE
BUSINESS BUT I
MANAGED TO KEEP THE
WEBSITE ADDRESS AND
THAT'S DOMAIN THING.

DOES MY BRAND
NEW SMILE
DENTURE EGO?

THANK YOU, MY
ARMS, FOR ALWAYS
BEING THERE BY
MY SIDE.

THE ARTIST THOUGHT
HIS FAVORITE PAINT
HAD BEEN STOLEN, BUT
IT WAS JUST A PIGMENT
OF HIS IMAGINATION.

WHAT DO YOU CALL
A COW WITH
TWO LEGS?

LEAN BEEF.

I TOOK UP FENCING.
BUT THE POLICE
INSIST I HAVE TO
GIVE IT BACK.

I CAN CUT WOOD BY
JUST LOOKING AT IT.
IT'S TRUE! I SAW IT
WITH MY OWN EYES.

KIDS WHO DON'T
LEARN TO TIE THEIR
SHOES PROPERLY ARE
BOUND TO WIND UP
ON THE KNOTTY LIST.

I DIDN'T USE TO
LIKE DUCT-TAPE
AT FIRST, BUT I
SOON BECAME
ATTACHED TO IT.

I COULDN'T BELIEVE THAT THE HIGHWAY DEPARTMENT CALLED MY DAD A THIEF BUT WHEN I GOT HOME, ALL THE SIGNS WERE THERE.

THE WEIGH-IN AT THE SUMO WRESTLING CHAMPIONSHIP WAS A LARGE SCALE EFFORT.

THE TIME MACHINE AND I GO WAY BACK.

I WAS GETTING INTO MY
CAR THE OTHER DAY
AND A MAN SAID "CAN
YOU GIVE ME A LIFT?"

I SAID, "SURE, YOU LOOK
GREAT, CHASE YOUR
DREAMS, GO FOR IT!"

ACUPUNCTURE IS A
JAB WELL DONE.

WHEN A CLOCK
IS STILL HUNGRY,
IT GOES BACK
FOUR SECONDS.

THE GIRL QUIT HER
JOB AT THE DONUT
FACTORY BECAUSE
SHE WAS FED UP WITH
THE HOLE BUSINESS.

THE IRISH ARE
WEALTHY SINCE
THEIR CAPITOL IS
ALWAYS DUBLIN.

I LIFT WEIGHTS ONLY
ON SATURDAY AND
SUNDAY BECAUSE
MONDAY TO FRIDAY
ARE WEAK DAYS.

I'VE GOT A CHICKEN-PROOF GARDEN. IT'S COMPLETELY IMPECCABLE!

TWO LOAFS OF BREAD WANTED TO GET MARRIED, WHICH IS WHY THEY ELOAFED.

THE PHARAOHS OF EGYPT CAME UP WITH THE FIRST PYRAMID SCHEME.

A HAIR-RAISING
EXPERIENCE
SOUNDS PROMISING
TO A BALD MAN.

MY WIFE LIKES IT
WHEN I BLOW AIR
ON HER WHEN SHE'S
HOT, BUT HONESTLY...
I'M NOT A FAN.

YOU CAN'T PLAY
CARDS ON A SMALL
BOAT BECAUSE
SOMEONE IS ALWAYS
HITTING THE DECK.

I REMEMBER BEING
IN SO MUCH DEBT
THAT I COULDN'T
AFFORD MY
ELECTRICITY BILLS,
IT WAS A DARK TIME.

NEVER DATE A
TENNIS PLAYER.
LOVE MEANS
NOTHING TO THEM.

I WAS GOING TO BUY
A BOOK ON PHOBIAS,
BUT I WAS AFRAID IT
WOULDN'T HELP ME.

I DECIDED TO BECOME
A PROFESSIONAL
FISHERMAN, BUT
DISCOVERED THAT
I COULDN'T LIVE ON
MY NET INCOME.

TODAY I HAVE MET
THE VEGETARIAN
BROTHER OF BRUCE
LEE. BROCCO LEE.

TOILET PAPER
PLAYS AN
IMPORTANT ROLL
IN MY LIFE.

A MUSHROOM WALKS INTO A BAR AND ORDERS A DRINK. THE BARTENDER TELLS HIM TO GET OUT.

THE MUSHROOM SAYS, "WHY? I'M A FUN-GUY."

I USED TO BE A BAKER, BUT I DIDN'T MAKE ENOUGH DOUGH.

GETTING PAID TO SLEEP WOULD BE A DREAM JOB.

I DID A THEATRICAL
PERFORMANCE ABOUT
PUNS. REALLY IT
WAS JUST A PLAY
ON WORDS.

LAST WEEK I
CALLED SOMEONE A
WATERING HOLE BUT
I MEANT WELL.

I DON'T WANT
TO CUT MY HAIR!
I'M REALLY
ATTACHED TO IT.

I GOOGLED, "HOW TO START A CAMPFIRE." I GOT 49,000 MATCHES.

WHEN MY GIRLFRIEND ASKED ME TO STOP IMPERSONATING A FLAMINGO, I HAD TO PUT MY FOOT DOWN.

REGULAR VISITORS TO THE DENTIST ARE FAMILIAR WITH THE DRILL.

THIS GRAVITY JOKE
IS GETTING A BIT
OLD, BUT I FALL FOR
IT EVERY TIME.

DID YOU HEAR ABOUT
THE KIDNAPPING
AT SCHOOL?

IT'S OKAY.
HE WOKE UP.

ENGLAND DOESN'T HAVE
A KIDNEY BANK, BUT IT
DOES HAVE A LIVERPOOL.

MY FRIEND ASKED ME
HOW I BAKE MY BREAD.
I SAID I COULDN'T TELL
HIM BECAUSE IT WAS ON
A KNEAD TO KNOW BASIS.

I WONDERED WHY
THE BASEBALL WAS
GETTING BIGGER.
THEN IT HIT ME.

I'M READING A BOOK
ABOUT ANTI-GRAVITY.
IT'S IMPOSSIBLE
TO PUT DOWN.

A PAIR OF JUMPER CABLES WALK INTO A BAR AND ASK FOR A DRINK. THE BARTENDER SAYS, "OK, BUT I DON'T WANT YOU STARTING ANYTHING IN HERE."

TO WRITE WITH A BROKEN PENCIL IS POINTLESS.

I WANNA MAKE A JOKE ABOUT SODIUM, BUT NA..

AS A WIZARD, I ENJOY
TURNING OBJECTS
INTO A GLASS. JUST
WANTED TO MAKE
THAT CLEAR.

A BICYCLE CAN'T
STAND ON ITS
OWN BECAUSE IT'S
TWO TIRED.

I'VE JUST WRITTEN
A SONG ABOUT
TORTILLAS-
ACTUALLY, IT'S
MORE OF A RAP.

THE PILOT WAS A
LONER BUT EVEN
FOR HIM FLYING A
DRONE WAS SIMPLY
TOO REMOTE.

I MANAGED TO GET
A GOOD JOB FOR A
POOL MAINTENANCE
COMPANY, BUT THE
WORK WAS JUST
TOO DRAINING.

WITH GREAT REFLEXES
COMES GREAT
RESPONSE ABILITY.

TODAY AT THE BANK,
AN OLD LADY ASKED
ME TO HELP CHECK
HER BALANCE...

SO I PUSHED
HER OVER.

TWO WINDMILLS
ARE STANDING IN A
FIELD AND ONE ASKS
THE OTHER, "WHAT
KIND OF MUSIC
DO YOU LIKE?"

THE OTHER SAYS, "I'M
A BIG METAL FAN."

THIEVES HAD BROKEN
INTO MY HOUSE AND
STOLEN EVERYTHING
EXCEPT MY SOAP,
SHOWER GEL, TOWELS
AND DEODORANT.
DIRTY BASTARDS.

WHEN I GET NAKED
IN THE BATHROOM,
THE SHOWER USUALLY
GETS TURNED ON.

MY COMPUTER'S GOT
MILEY VIRUS. IT HAS
STOPPED TWERKING.

I RECENTLY GOT CRUSHED BY A PILE OF BOOKS, BUT I SUPPOSE I'VE ONLY GOT MY SHELF TO BLAME.

I COULDN'T QUITE REMEMBER HOW TO THROW A BOOMERANG, BUT EVENTUALLY, IT CAME BACK TO ME.

LAST TIME I GOT CAUGHT STEALING A CALENDAR I GOT 12 MONTHS.

I THOUGHT ABOUT
GOING ON AN
ALL-ALMOND DIET.

BUT THAT'S JUST NUTS!

OLD ARTISTS NEVER
RETIRE, THEY
WITHDRAW INSTEAD!

IF YOU EVER GET
COLD, JUST STAND IN A
CORNER FOR A BIT...

THEY'RE USUALLY
AROUND 90 DEGREES.

A MAN KNOCKED
ON MY DOOR AND
ASKED FOR A SMALL
DONATION FOR A LOCAL
SWIMMING POOL.
SO I GAVE HIM A
GLASS OF WATER.

MASKS HAVE NO
FACE VALUE.

A DOG GAVE BIRTH
TO PUPPIES AT
THE ROADSIDE
AND WAS FINED
FOR LITTERING.

IF A CHILD REFUSES
TO SLEEP DURING
NAP TIME, ARE
THEY GUILTY OF
RESISTING A REST?

I'M NOT A HUGE
FAN OF ARCHERY.
IT WAS WAY TOO
MANY DRAWBACKS!

I GET DISTRACTED
BY ALL THE MEATS IN
THE DELI SECTION,
MUST BE MY SHORT
ATTENTION SPAM.

I WAS GOING TO
TELL MY PIZZA JOKE
BUT I THINK IT'S A
BIT TOO CHEESY.

THE LIBRARIAN
DIDN'T KNOW WHAT
TO DO WITH THE BOOK
ABOUT TESLA'S LOVE
OF ELECTRICITY, SO
HE FILED IT UNDER
'CURRENT AFFAIRS.'

BRITAIN IS A WET
PLACE DUE TO THE
QUEEN'S LONG REIGN.

I SAW AN AD FOR
BURIAL PLOTS, AND
THOUGHT TO MYSELF
THIS IS THE LAST
THING I NEED.

JUST BURNED 2,000
CALORIES. THAT'S THE
LAST TIME I LEAVE
BROWNIES IN THE
OVEN WHILE I NAP.

I USED TO HATE MATH
UNTIL I REALIZED
THAT DECIMALS
HAVE A POINT.

I GOT A NEW PAIR OF GLOVES TODAY, BUT THEY'RE BOTH 'LEFTS' WHICH, ON THE ONE HAND, IS GREAT, BUT ON THE OTHER, IT'S JUST NOT RIGHT.

ONCE YOU CONTRACT AN INFECTION OF THE BLADDER, URINE TROUBLE.

I THOUGHT ABOUT BECOMING A WITCH, SO I TRIED IT OUT FOR A SPELL.

I TOLD MY GIRLFRIEND
SHE DREW HER
EYEBROWS TOO HIGH.
SHE SEEMED
SURPRISED.

ATHEISM IS A
NON-PROPHET
ORGANIZATION.

MY TENNIS OPPONENT
WAS NOT TOO
HAPPY WITH MY
SERVES, HE KEPT
RETURNING THEM.

I CAN'T BELIEVE I GOT FIRED FROM THE CALENDAR FACTORY. ALL I DID WAS TAKE A DAY OFF.

OUR OFFICE DEFIBRILLATOR DIDN'T WORK. NOBODY WAS SHOCKED.

I SAW A DOCUMENTARY ON HOW SHIPS ARE KEPT TOGETHER. IT WAS RIVETING!

I WORKED IN THE WOODS
AS A LUMBERJACK,
BUT I JUST COULDN'T
HACK IT, SO THEY
GAVE ME THE AX.

THE NEWSPAPER'S
RATIONALE FOR
RUNNING THE STORY
WAS PAPER THIN.

SUE BROKE HER
FINGER TODAY,
BUT ON THE OTHER
HAND SHE WAS
COMPLETELY FINE.

WHAT DOES A BLANKET
SAY WHEN IT FALLS OFF
THE BED? OH SHEET!

I'M ALWAYS GETTING
RUN OVER BY THE SAME
BIKE, SAME DAY EVERY
MONTH, SAME PLACE,
MONTH AFTER MONTH.

IT'S A VICIOUS CYCLE.

I'M WORKING ON A
DEVICE THAT WILL READ
MINDS. I'D LOVE TO
HEAR YOUR THOUGHTS.

ABOUT A MONTH BEFORE HE DIED, MY UNCLE HAD HIS BACK COVERED IN LARD. AFTER THAT, HE WENT DOWN HILL FAST.

THE SOLDIER WHO SURVIVED MUSTARD GAS AND PEPPER SPRAY IS NOW A SEASONED VETERAN.

SHE WAS ONLY A WHISKEY MAKER, BUT I LOVED HER STILL.

THE CARPENTER
CAME AROUND THE
OTHER DAY. HE MADE
THE BEST ENTRANCE
I HAVE EVER SEEN...

NEVER LIE
TO AN X-RAY
TECHNICIAN. THEY
CAN SEE RIGHT
THROUGH YOU.

I PLANNED TO FIND
MY WATCH TODAY,
BUT I DIDN'T
HAVE THE TIME.

I'VE BEEN
LEARNING BRAILLE.
I'M SURE I'LL
MASTER IT ONCE I
GET A FEEL FOR IT.

I OFTEN SAY TO
MYSELF, "I CAN'T
BELIEVE THAT CLONING
MACHINE WORKED!"

MY FRIEND ASKED
ME TO SHIP HIM
A TRUCKLOAD OF
FOOD BUT IT JUST
WASN'T PALATABLE.

IF YOU JUMPED OFF
A BRIDGE IN PARIS,
YOU'D BE IN SEINE.

I SAW AN
ADVERTISEMENT THAT
READ: "TELEVISION
FOR SALE, $1, VOLUME
STUCK ON FULL. "

I THOUGHT TO MYSELF, I
CAN'T TURN THAT DOWN.

A BOILED EGG IN
THE MORNING IS
HARD TO BEAT.

A RUBBER BAND PISTOL WAS CONFISCATED FROM ALGEBRA CLASS, BECAUSE IT WAS A WEAPON OF MATH DISRUPTION.

FOR HALLOWEEN WE DRESSED UP AS ALMONDS. EVERYONE COULD TELL WE WERE NUTS.

I'M LOOKING FOR SOME GOOD FISH JOKES. IF YOU KNOW ANY, LET MINNOW.

THANKS FOR EXPLAINING THE WORD "MANY" TO ME, IT MEANS A LOT.

DID YOU HEAR ABOUT THE GUY WHO GOT HIT IN THE HEAD WITH A CAN OF SODA?

HE WAS LUCKY IT WAS A SOFT DRINK.

DON'T DRINK WITH GHOSTS, THEY CAN'T HANDLE THEIR BOOS.

I COME FROM A
FAMILY OF FAILED
MAGICIANS. I HAVE
TWO HALF-SISTERS.

I'D TELL YOU A
REALLY GOOD JOKE
ABOUT CLOUDS. BUT
I'M AFRAID IT'S WAY
OVER YOUR HEAD.

SOMEONE STOLE
ALL MY LAMPS.
I COULDN'T BE
MORE DELIGHTED.

I'D TELL YOU MY
CONSTRUCTION
JOKE BUT I'M STILL
WORKING ON IT.

I'D LOVE TO KNOW HOW
THE EARTH ROTATES.
IT WOULD TOTALLY
MAKE MY DAY.

SANG THE RAINBOW
SONG IN FRONT OF
A POLICE OFFICER,
GOT ARRESTED FOR
COLORFUL LANGUAGE.

IF A SHORT PSYCHIC
BROKE OUT OF
JAIL, THEN YOU'D
HAVE A SMALL
MEDIUM AT LARGE.

TWO CHEESE TRUCKS
RAN INTO EACH
OTHER. DE BRIE
WAS EVERYWHERE.

I ALWAYS WANTED
TO LEARN TO
PROCRASTINATE...
JUST NEVER GOT
AROUND TO IT.

JOKES ABOUT
UNEMPLOYED PEOPLE
ARE NOT FUNNY. THEY
JUST DON'T WORK.

TENNIS IS ONE
OF THE NOISIEST
SPORTS TO WATCH
BECAUSE EACH
PLAYER RAISES
A RACKET.

MY NEW GIRLFRIEND
WORKS AT THE
ZOO. I THINK SHE
IS A KEEPER.

IF THE RIGHT SIDE OF
THE BRAIN CONTROLS
THE LEFT SIDE OF THE
BODY, THEN LEFTIES
ARE THE ONLY ONES IN
THEIR RIGHT MIND.

REFUSING TO GO TO
THE GYM COUNTS
AS RESISTANCE
TRAINING, RIGHT?

THE CARDIOVASCULAR
SYSTEM IS A WORK
OF ARTERY, BUT IT IS
ALSO PRETTY VEIN.

AFTER A LONG
TIME WAITING
FOR THE BOWLING
ALLEY TO OPEN, WE
EVENTUALLY GOT
THE BALL ROLLING.

I'D LOVE TO
VISIT HOLLAND,
WOODEN SHOE?

I COULDN'T WORK OUT
HOW TO FASTEN MY
SEATBELT FOR AGES.
BUT THEN ONE DAY,
IT JUST CLICKED.

I GAVE ALL MY DEAD
BATTERIES AWAY...

THEY WERE FREE
OF CHARGE!

IT WAS COLD IN
THE BEDROOM SO
I LAID DOWN IN
THE FIREPLACE AND
SLEPT LIKE A LOG.

I UNDERSTAND HOW
GEMS ARE MADE. THE
CONCEPT IS CRYSTAL
CLEAR TO ME.

THERE WAS A BIG
PADDLE SALE AT
THE BOAT STORE.
IT WAS QUITE
AN OAR DEAL.

I'VE ACCIDENTALLY
SWALLOWED SOME
SCRABBLE TILES. MY
NEXT POOP COULD
SPELL DISASTER.

MY FRIEND'S BAKERY
BURNED DOWN LAST
NIGHT. NOW HIS
BUSINESS IS TOAST.

I LOVE
SWITZERLAND! I'M
NOT SURE WHAT THE
BEST THING ABOUT
IT IS, BUT THEIR
FLAG IS A BIG PLUS.

FIXING BROKEN
WINDOWS IS A PANE
IN THE GLASS.

SOMEONE STOLE MY
TOILET PAPER AND
THE POLICE HAVE
NOTHING TO GO ON.

I ACCIDENTALLY SHOT SOMEONE WITH A STARTING GUN THE OTHER DAY. I'VE BEEN CHARGED WITH A RACE CRIME.

A PET STORE HAD A BIRD CONTEST WITH NO PERCHES NECESSARY.

I DON'T TRUST STAIRS. THEY'RE ALWAYS UP TO SOMETHING.